JUMPING AHEAD
YOUNG AND GIFTED SERIES

THIS BOOK BELONGS TO:

_____

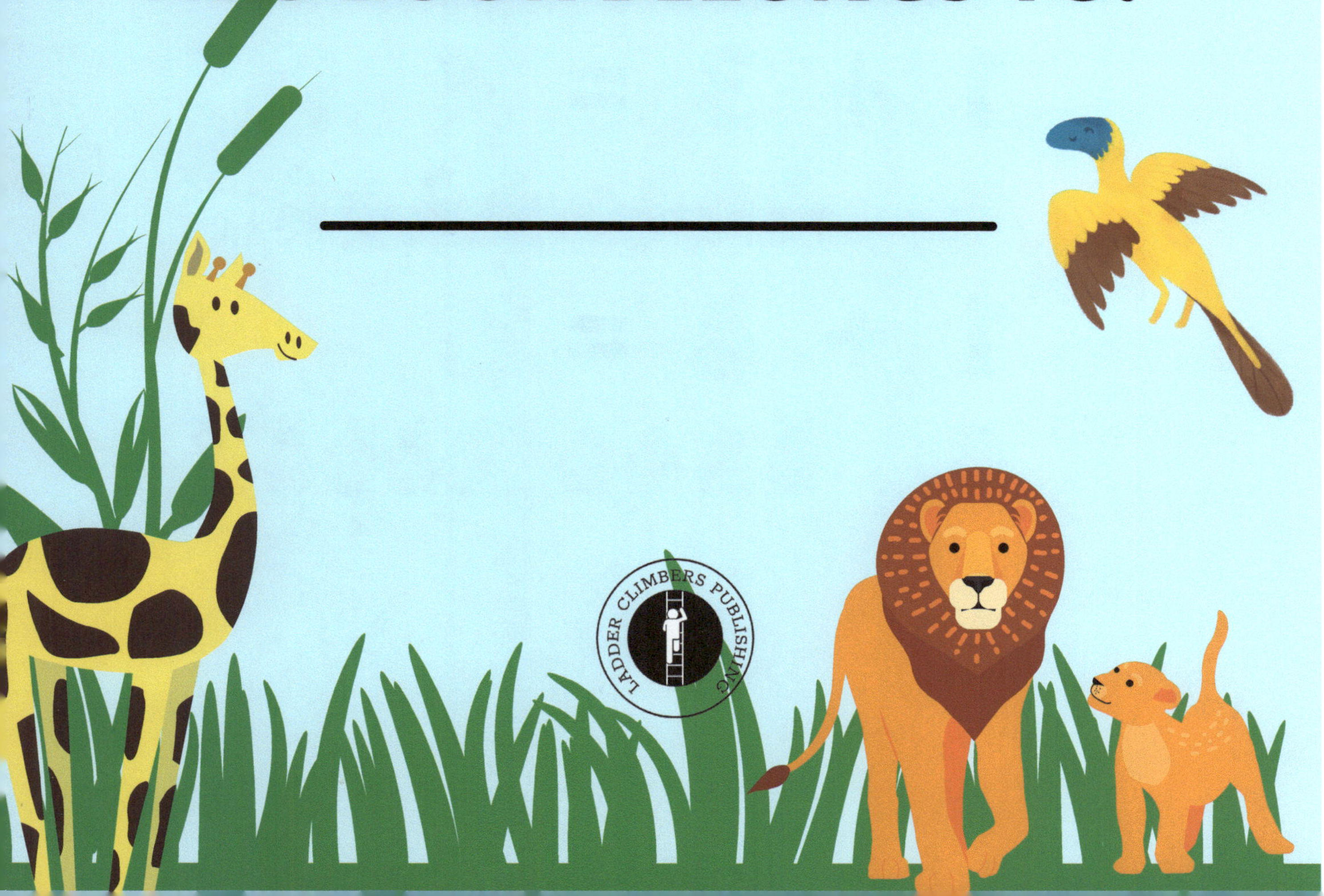

ADDING

ADDING, SOMETIMES CALLED PLUS, CAN BE REALLY EXCITING TO LEARN. COUNT THE NUMBER OF LADYBUGS TO GET THE ANSWER.

1 + 1 = 2

1 + 2 = 3

1 + 3 = 4

1 + 4 = 5

ADDING

TRY IT YOURSELF

ADDING, SOMETIMES CALLED PLUS, CAN BE REALLY EXCITING TO LEARN. COUNT THE NUMBER OF POPSICLES TO GET THE ANSWER.

$1 + 5 = \underline{\quad}$

$1 + 6 = \underline{\quad}$

$1 + 7 = \underline{\quad}$

$1 + 8 = \underline{\quad}$

ADDING

TRY IT YOURSELF

ADDING, SOMETIMES CALLED PLUS, CAN BE REALLY EXCITING TO LEARN. COUNT THE NUMBER OF COOKIES TO GET THE ANSWER.

$$1 + 9 = \underline{\quad}$$

$$1 + 10 = \underline{\quad}$$

$$1 + 11 = \underline{\quad}$$

$$1 + 12 = \underline{\quad}$$

ADDING

ADDING, SOMETIMES CALLED PLUS, CAN BE REALLY EXCITING TO LEARN. COUNT THE NUMBER OF GINGERBREAD COOKIES TO GET THE ANSWER.

$$2 + 1 = 3$$

$$2 + 2 = 4$$

$$2 + 3 = 5$$

$$2 + 4 = 6$$

ADDING

ADDING, SOMETIMES CALLED PLUS, CAN BE REALLY EXCITING TO LEARN. COUNT THE NUMBER OF LOLLIPOPS TO GET THE ANSWER.

$$2 + 5 = \underline{}$$

$$2 + 6 = \underline{}$$

$$2 + 7 = \underline{}$$

$$2 + 8 = \underline{}$$

ADDING

TRY IT YOURSELF

ADDING, SOMETIMES CALLED PLUS, CAN BE REALLY EXCITING TO LEARN. COUNT THE NUMBER OF PUPPIES TO GET THE ANSWER.

$$2 + 9 = \underline{\quad}$$

$$2 + 10 = \underline{\quad}$$

$$2 + 11 = \underline{\quad}$$

$$2 + 12 = \underline{\quad}$$

SUBTRACTING

SUBTRACTING, SOMETIMES CALLED MINUS OR TAKEAWAY, CAN BE FUN BUT TRICKY. HERE IS AN EASIER WAY TO LEARN HOW TO TAKE AWAY.

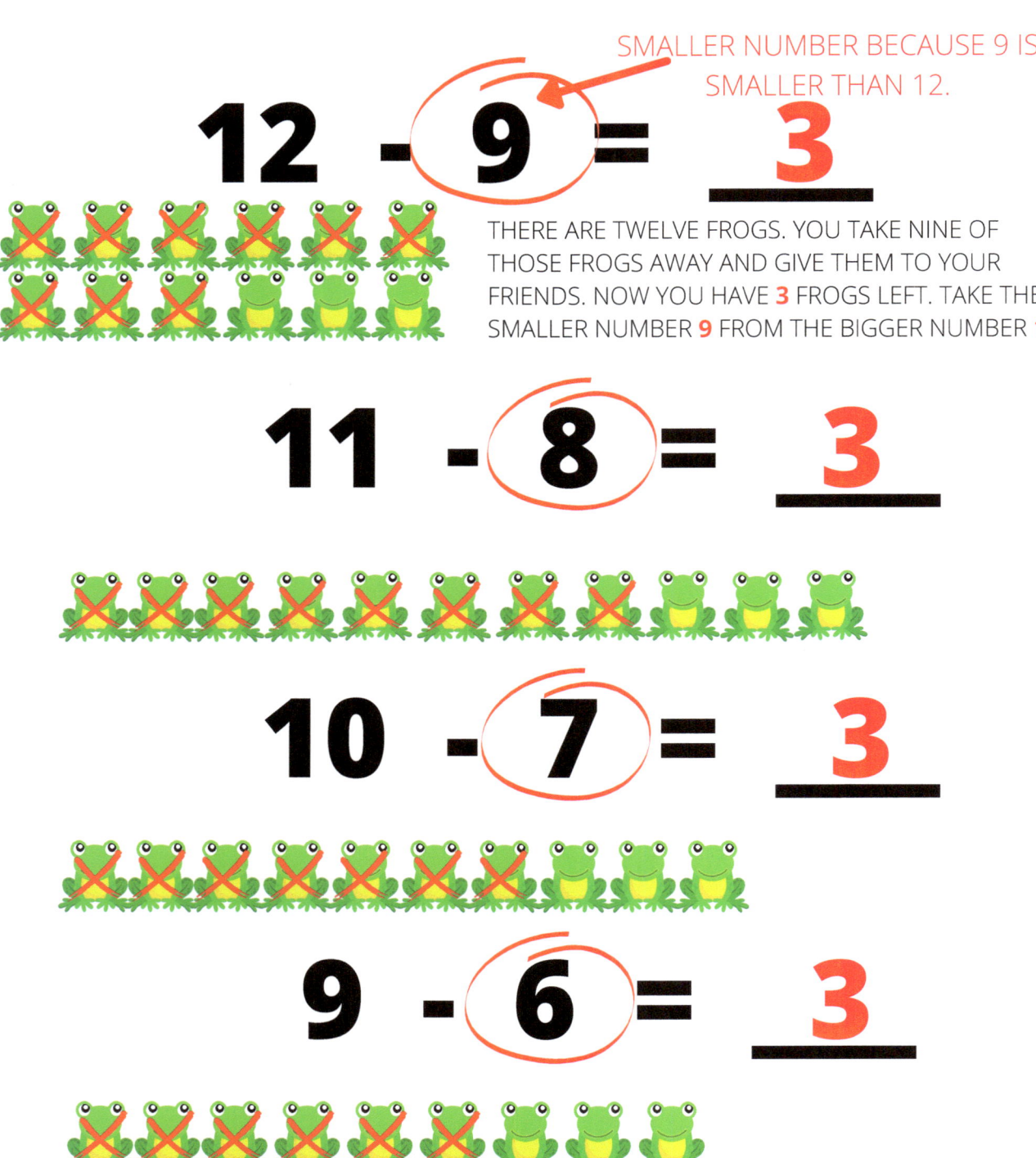

SMALLER NUMBER BECAUSE 9 IS SMALLER THAN 12.

12 - 9 = 3

THERE ARE TWELVE FROGS. YOU TAKE NINE OF THOSE FROGS AWAY AND GIVE THEM TO YOUR FRIENDS. NOW YOU HAVE **3** FROGS LEFT. TAKE THE SMALLER NUMBER **9** FROM THE BIGGER NUMBER **12**.

11 - 8 = 3

10 - 7 = 3

9 - 6 = 3

SUBTRACTING   TRY IT YOURSELF

SUBTRACTING, SOMETIMES CALLED MINUS OR TAKEAWAY, CAN BE FUN BUT TRICKY. TAKE AWAY THE AMOUNT OF CUPCAKES BY CROSSING OUT THE SMALLER NUMBERS.

8 - 1 = ___

7 - 2 = ___

6 - 3 = ___

5 - 4 = ___

SUBTRACTING

SUBTRACTING, SOMETIMES CALLED MINUS OR TAKEAWAY, CAN BE FUN BUT TRICKY. TAKE AWAY THE AMOUNT OF MILK CARTONS BY CROSSING OUT THE SMALLER NUMBERS.

$$4 - 3 = \underline{}$$

$$3 - 2 = \underline{}$$

$$2 - 1 = \underline{}$$

$$1 - 0 = \underline{}$$

COINS

LEARN THE VALUE OF COINS. BELOW IS THE COIN AND VALUE FOR EACH.

PENNY = 1¢

NICKEL = 5¢

DIME = 10¢

QUARTER = 25¢

COUNT THE PENNIES BY 1'S

COUNT EACH LINE AND WRITE YOUR ANSWER

= _____ ¢

= _____ ¢

= _____ ¢

= _____ ¢

= _____ ¢

= _____ ¢

COUNT THE NICKELS BY 5'S

COUNT EACH LINE AND WRITE YOUR ANSWER

= _____ ¢

= _____ ¢

= _____ ¢

= _____ ¢

= _____ ¢

= _____ ¢

COUNT THE DIMES BY 10'S

COUNT EACH LINE AND WRITE YOUR ANSWER

= _____ ¢

= _____ ¢

= _____ ¢

= _____ ¢

= _____ ¢

= _____ ¢

COUNT QUARTERS BY 25'S

COUNT EACH LINE AND WRITE YOUR ANSWER

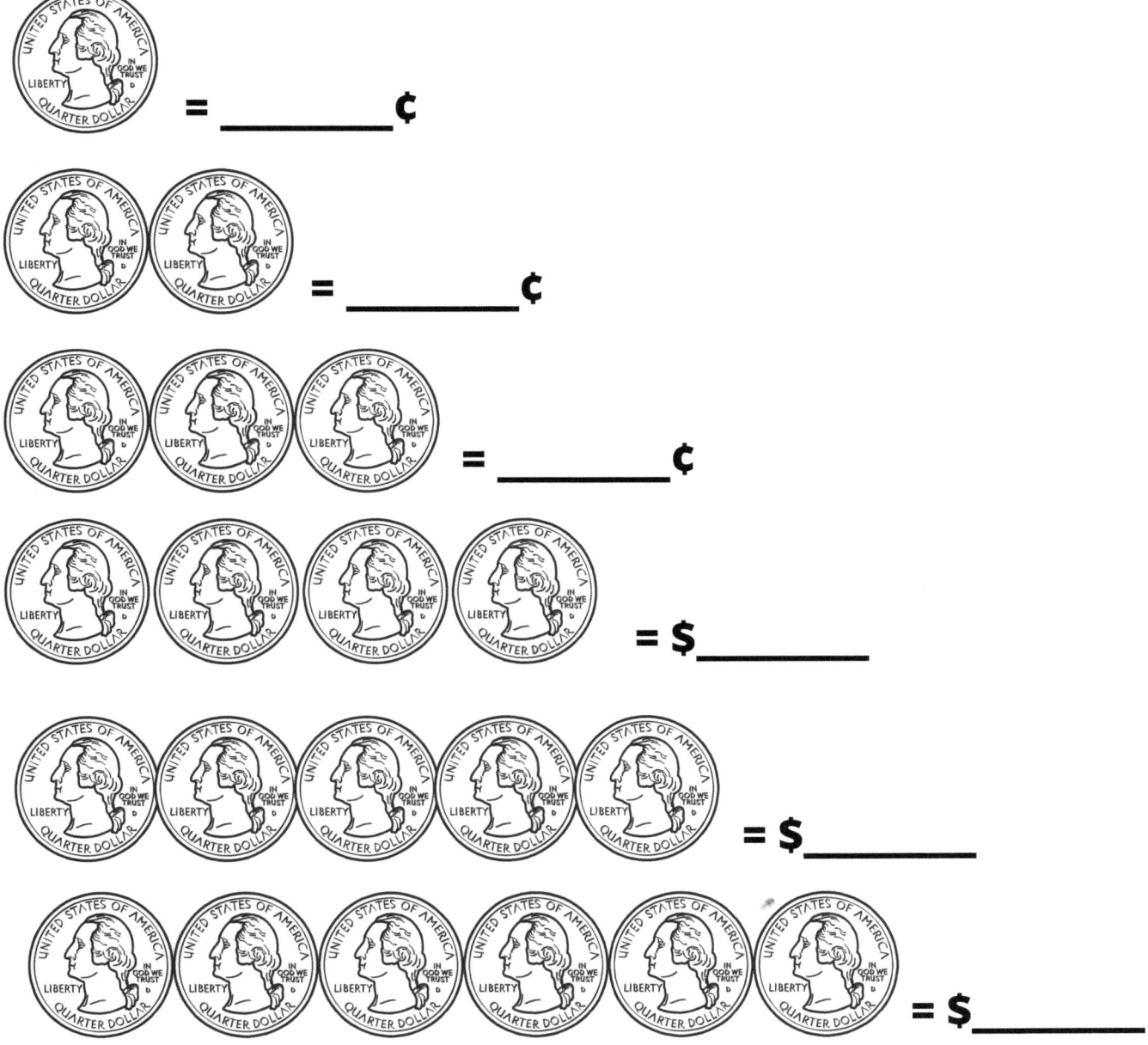

= _____¢

= _____¢

= _____¢

= $_____

= $_____

= $_____

HOW MUCH MONEY?

COUNT THE COINS AND WRITE THE TOTAL AMOUNT

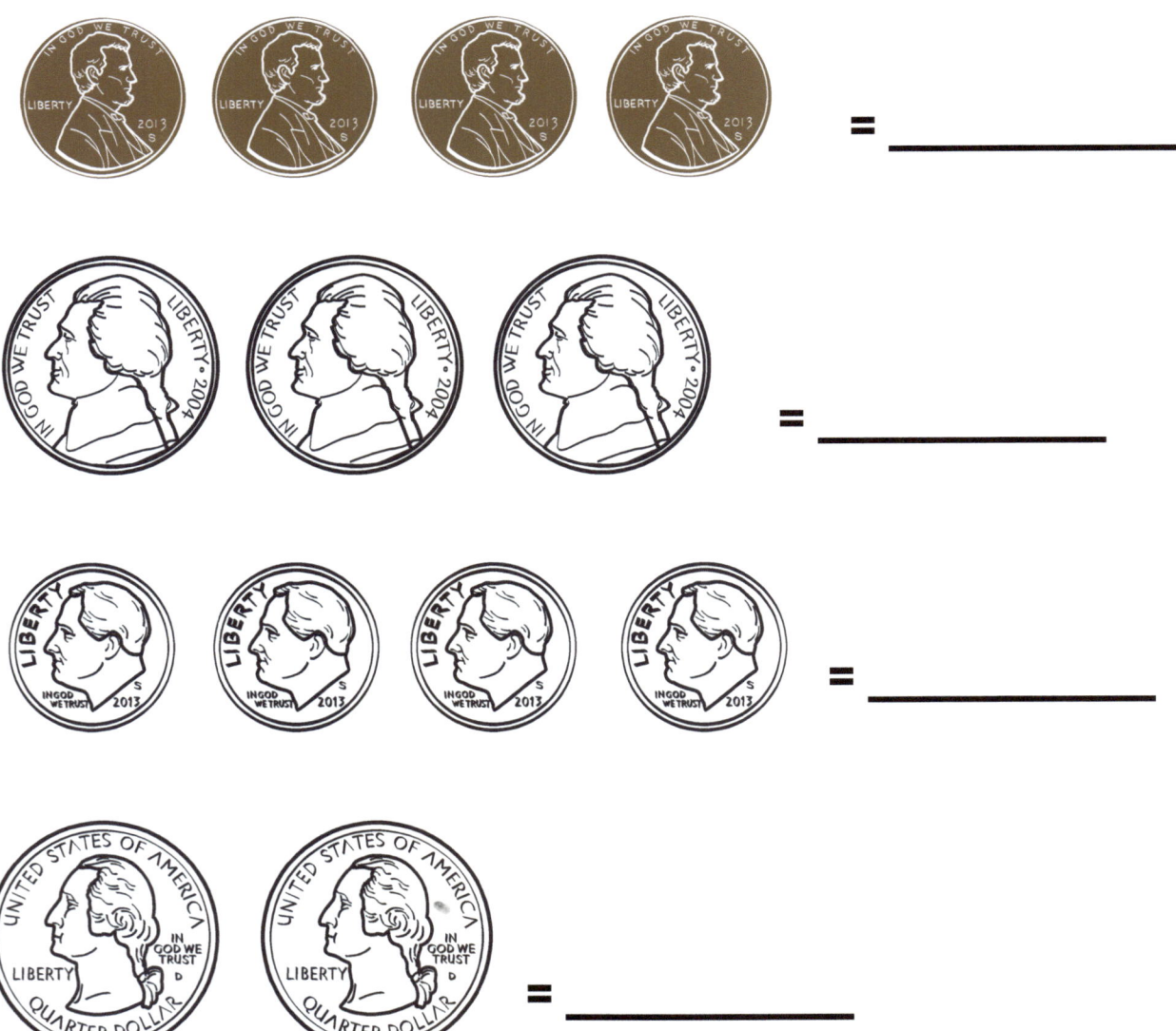

= _____

= _____

= _____

= _____

HOW MUCH MONEY?

COUNT THE COINS AND WRITE THE TOTAL AMOUNT

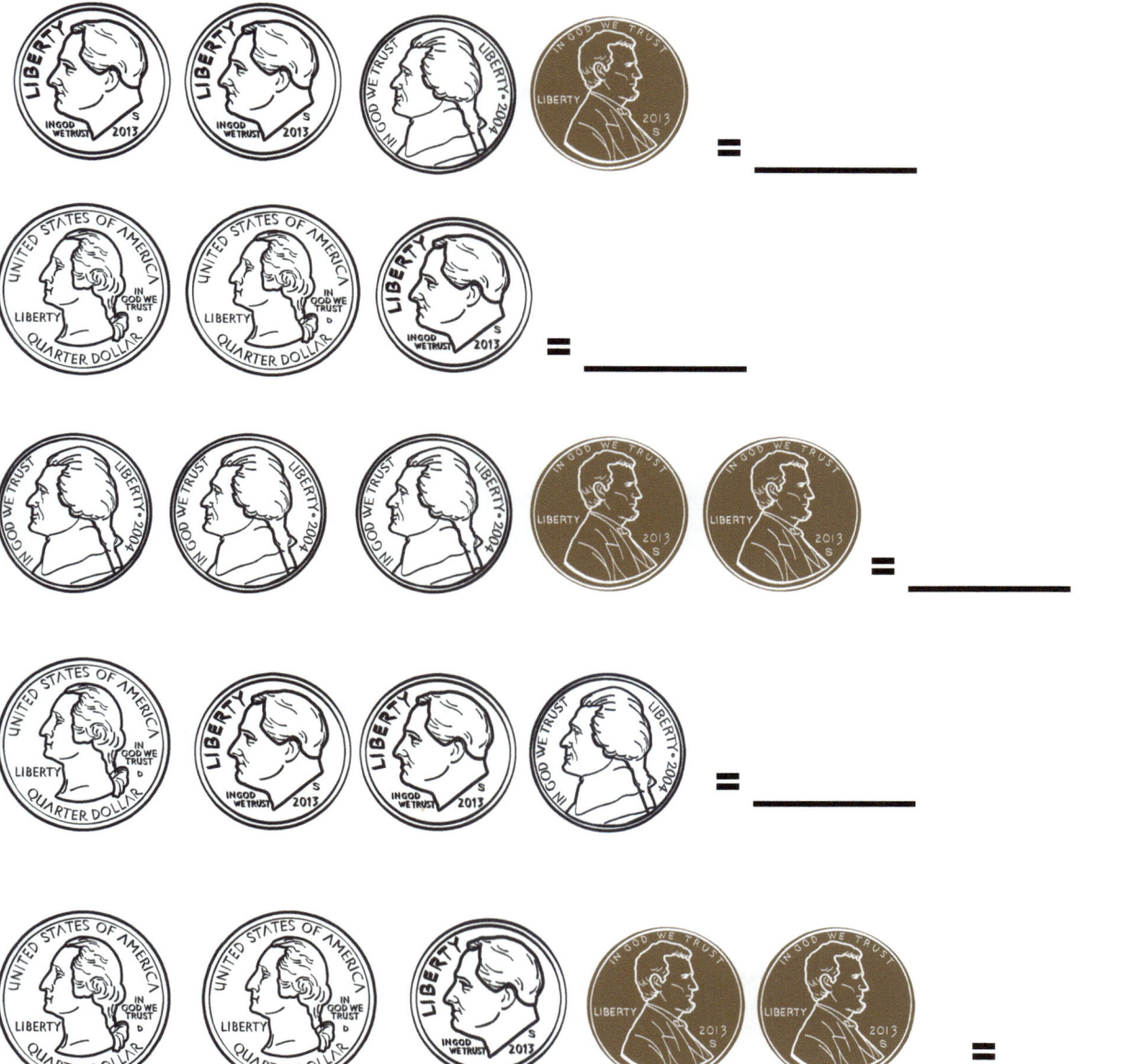

HOW MUCH MONEY?

COUNT THE COINS ON THE RIGHT SIDE AND THEN MATCH THEM TO THE ITEMS ON THE LEFT SIDE.

COUNTING MONEY

PAPER MONEY, CALLED DOLLARS, IS USED TO BUY THINGS WE NEED OR WANT. LEARN THE VALUE OF PAPER MONEY BELOW.

 **ONE DOLLAR BILL = $1.00**

 **FIVE DOLLAR BILL = $5.00**

 **TEN DOLLAR BILL = $10.00**

 **TWENTY DOLLAR BILL = $20.00**

 **FIFTY DOLLAR BILL = $50.00**

 **ONE HUNDRED DOLLAR BILL = $100.00**

COUNTING MONEY

COUNT THE DOLLARS AND WRITE THE TOTAL AMOUNT

$_____

$_____

$_____

COUNTING MONEY

COUNT THE DOLLARS ON THE RIGHT SIDE AND THEN MATCH THEM TO THE ITEMS ON THE LEFT SIDE.

$100.00

$10.00

$20.00

$50.00

TELLING TIME
ANALOG CLOCK

LEARNING HOW TO TELL TIME IS EXCITING. BELOW IS AN ANALOG CLOCK. IT HAS HANDS TO HELP YOU TELL THE TIME. THE LITTLE HAND (BLUE) TELLS THE HOUR AND THE BIG HAND (BLACK) TELLS THE MINUTES.

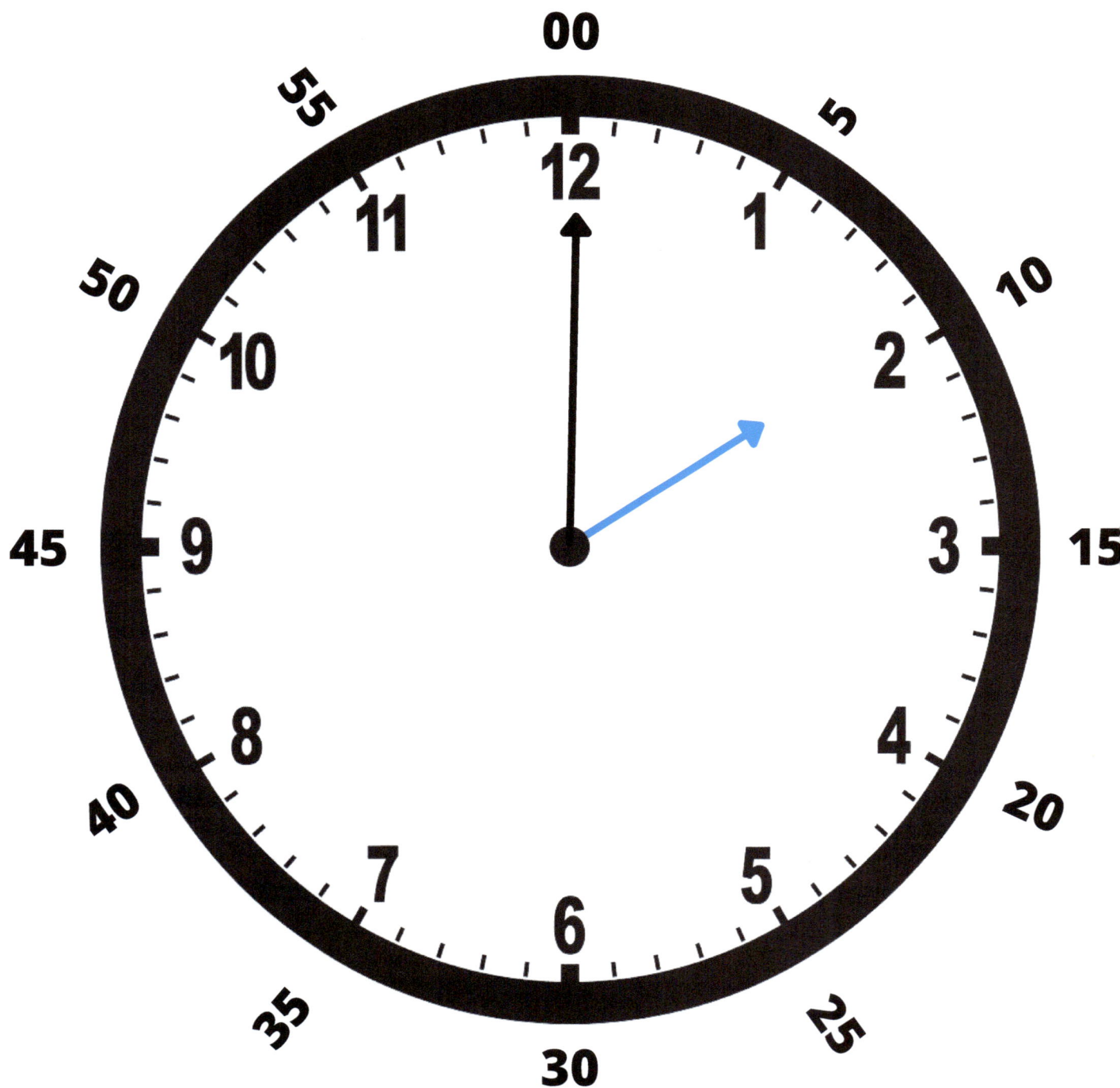

TELLING TIME
ANALOG CLOCKS

LEARNING HOW TO TELL TIME IS EXCITING. BELOW IS AN ANALOG CLOCK. IT HAS HANDS TO HELP YOU TELL THE TIME. THE LITTLE HAND (BLUE) TELLS THE HOUR AND THE BIG HAND (BLACK) TELLS THE MINUTES.

_____

_____

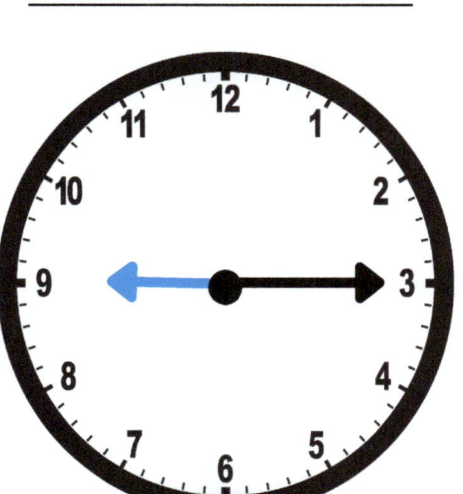

_____

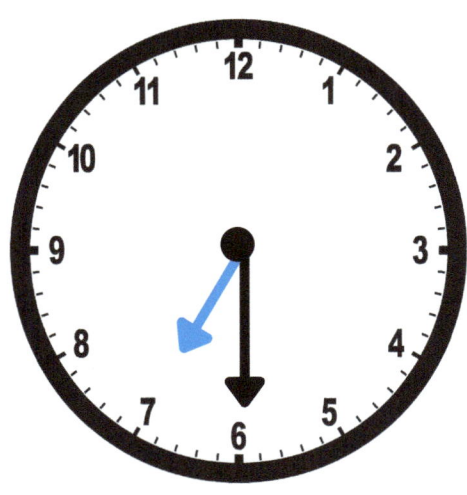

_____

TELLING TIME
ANALOG CLOCKS

LEARNING HOW TO TELL TIME IS EXCITING. BELOW IS AN ANALOG CLOCK. IT HAS HANDS TO HELP YOU TELL THE TIME. THE LITTLE HAND (BLUE) TELLS THE HOUR AND THE BIG HAND (BLACK) TELLS THE MINUTES.

_____

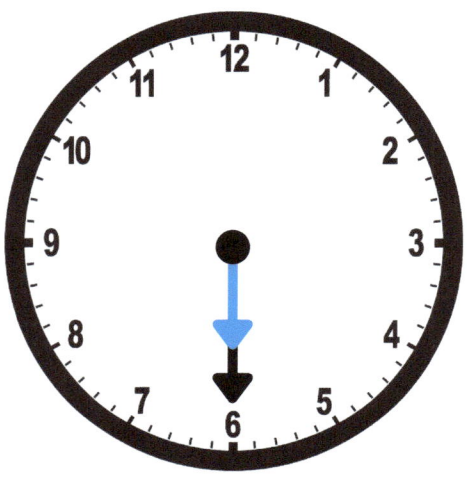

_____

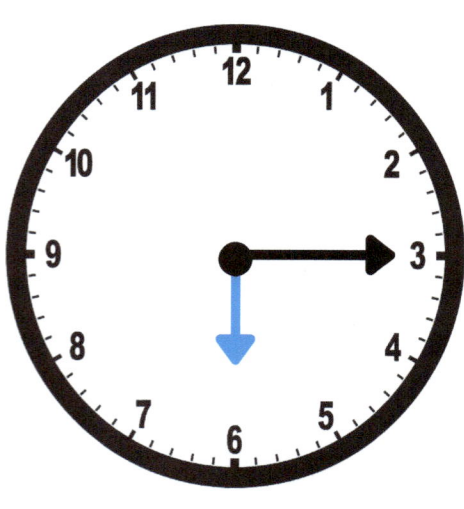

_____

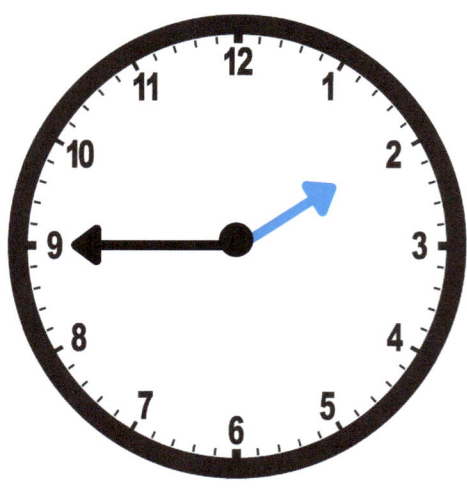

_____

TELLING TIME
DIGITAL CLOCK

DIGITAL CLOCKS SHOW THE HOUR BEFORE THE (:) AND THE MINUTES AFTER. WRITE THE TIME ON THE LINES BELOW THE CLOCKS

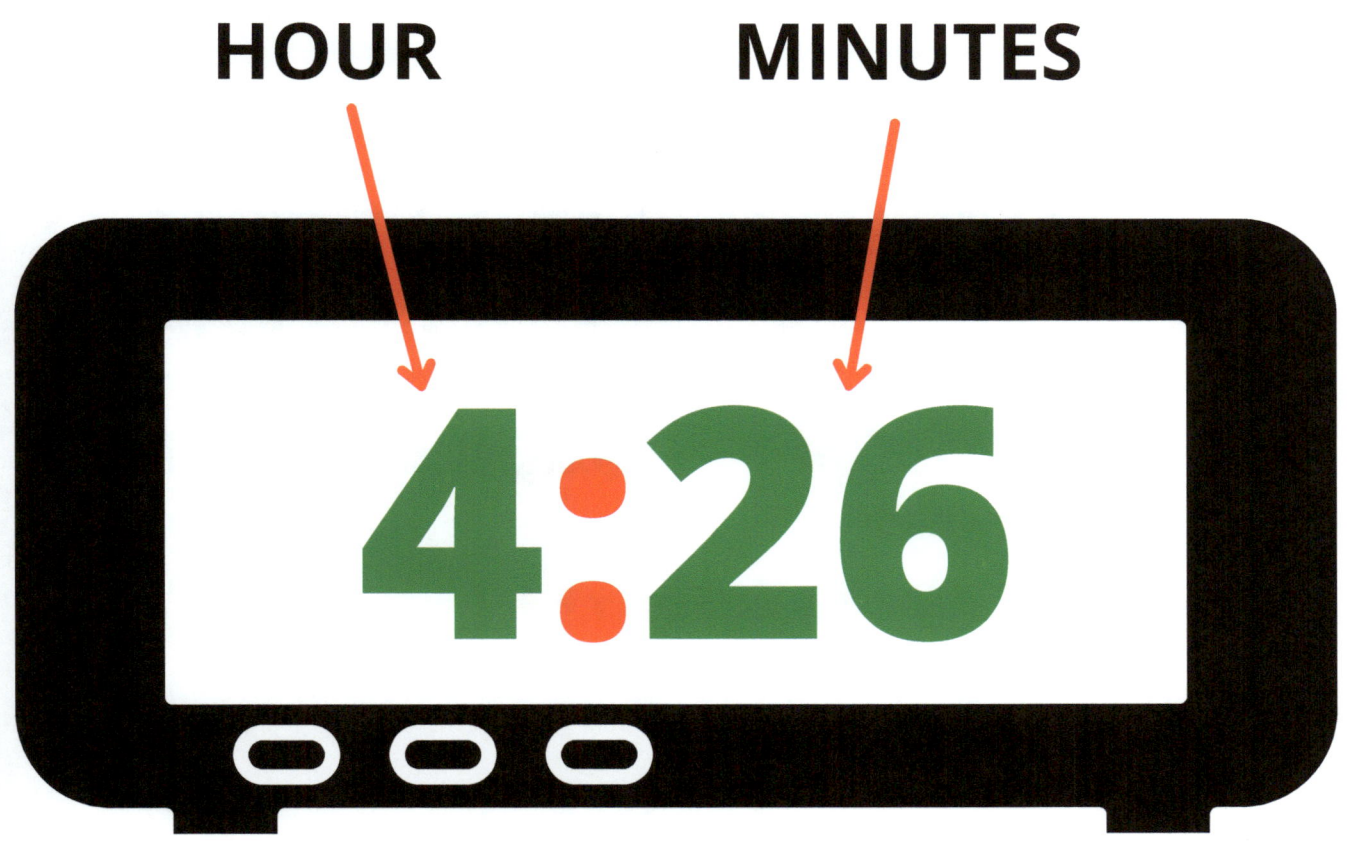

HOUR   MINUTES

TELLING TIME
DIGITAL CLOCK

DIGITAL CLOCKS SHOW THE HOUR BEFORE THE (:) AND THE MINUTES AFTER.
WRITE THE TIME ON THE LINES BELOW THE CLOCKS

_____

_____

_____

_____

ANSWER SECTION

ADDING

ADDING, SOMETIMES CALLED PLUS, CAN BE REALLY EXCITING TO LEARN. COUNT THE NUMBER OF POPSICLES TO GET THE ANSWER.

1 + 5 = 6

1 + 6 = 7

1 + 7 = 8

1 + 8 = 9

ADDING

ADDING, SOMETIMES CALLED PLUS, CAN BE REALLY EXCITING TO LEARN.
COUNT THE NUMBER OF COOKIES TO GET THE ANSWER.

1 + 9 = <u>10</u>

1 + 10 = <u>11</u>

1 + 11 = <u>12</u>

1 + 12 = <u>13</u>

ADDING

ADDING, SOMETIMES CALLED PLUS, CAN BE REALLY EXCITING TO LEARN.
COUNT THE NUMBER OF LOLLIPOPS TO GET THE ANSWER.

$$2 + 5 = \underline{7}$$

$$2 + 6 = \underline{8}$$

$$2 + 7 = \underline{9}$$

$$2 + 8 = \underline{10}$$

ADDING

ADDING, SOMETIMES CALLED PLUS, CAN BE REALLY EXCITING TO LEARN. COUNT THE NUMBER OF LOLLIPOPS TO GET THE ANSWER.

2 + 9 = 11

2 + 10 = 12

2 + 11 = 13

2 + 12 = 14

SUBTRACTING

SUBTRACTING, SOMETIMES CALLED MINUS OR TAKEAWAY, CAN BE FUN BUT TRICKY. TAKE AWAY THE AMOUNT OF CUPCAKES BY CROSSING OUT THE SMALLER NUMBERS.

$$8 - 1 = 7$$

$$7 - 2 = 5$$

$$6 - 3 = 3$$

$$5 - 4 = 1$$

SUBTRACTING

SUBTRACTING, SOMETIMES CALLED MINUS OR TAKEAWAY, CAN BE FUN BUT TRICKY. TAKE AWAY THE AMOUNT OF MILK CARTONS BY CROSSING OUT THE SMALLER NUMBERS.

4 - 3 = 1

3 - 2 = 1

2 - 1 = 1

1 - 0 = 1

COUNT THE PENNIES BY 1'S

COUNT EACH LINE AND WRITE YOUR ANSWER

= **1** ¢

= **2** ¢

= **3** ¢

= **4** ¢

= **5** ¢

= **6** ¢

COUNT THE NICKELS BY 5'S

COUNT EACH LINE AND WRITE YOUR ANSWER

= **5** ¢

= **10** ¢

= **15** ¢

= **20** ¢

= **25** ¢

= **30** ¢

COUNT THE DIMES BY 10'S

COUNT EACH LINE AND WRITE YOUR ANSWER

= __10__ ¢

= __20__ ¢

= __30__ ¢

= __40__ ¢

= __50__ ¢

= __60__ ¢

COUNT QUARTERS BY 25'S

COUNT EACH LINE AND WRITE YOUR ANSWER

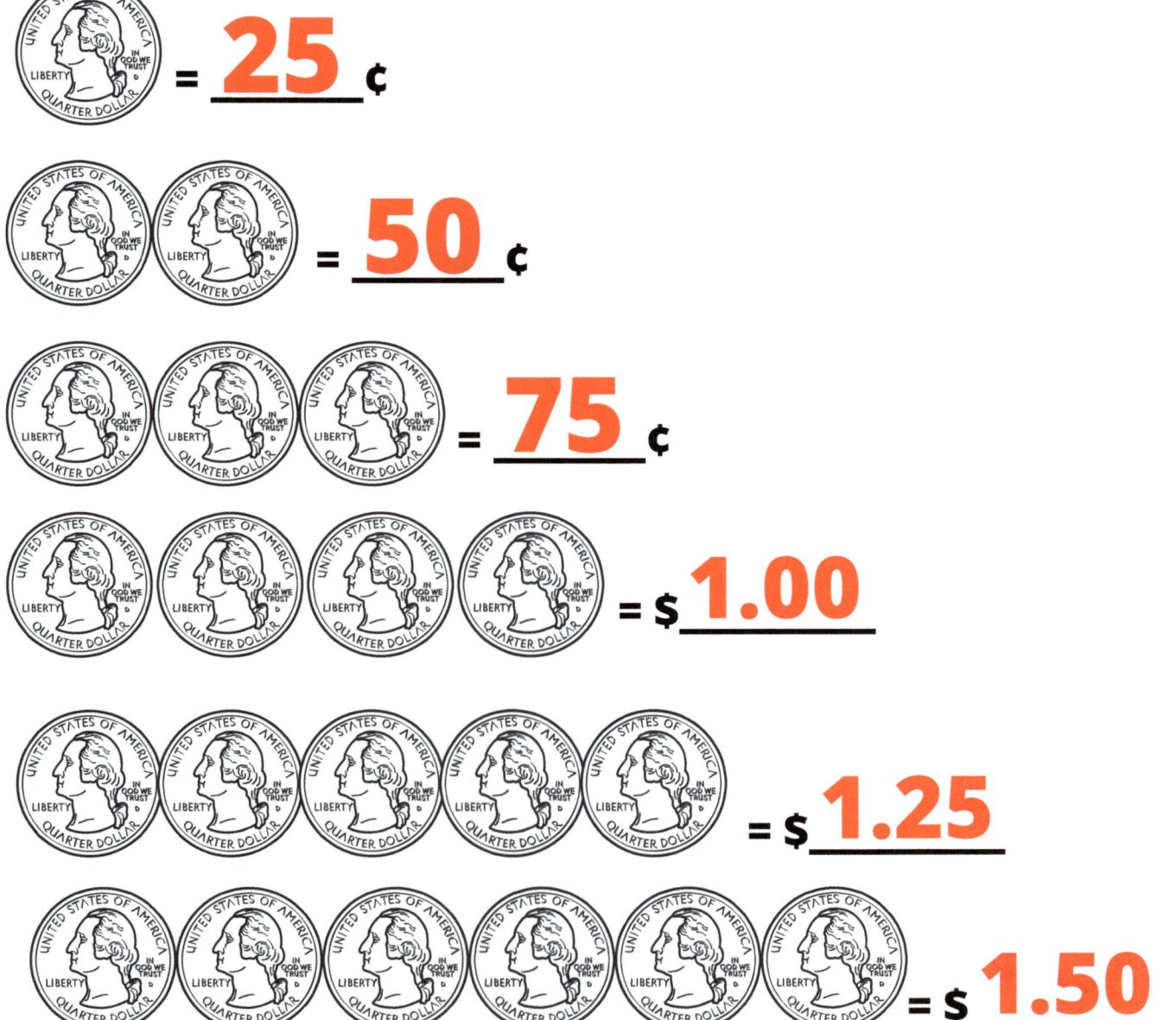

= **25** ¢

= **50** ¢

= **75** ¢

= $ **1.00**

= $ **1.25**

= $ **1.50**

HOW MUCH MONEY?

COUNT EACH LINE AND WRITE THE TOTAL AMOUNT

    =  **4¢**

   =  **15¢**

    =  **40¢**

  = **50¢**

HOW MUCH MONEY?

COUNT EACH LINE AND WRITE THE TOTAL AMOUNT

 = **26¢**

= **60¢**

 = **17¢**

= **50¢**

 = **62¢**

HOW MUCH MONEY?

COUNT THE COINS ON THE RIGHT SIDE AND THEN MATCH THEM TO THE ITEMS ON THE LEFT SIDE.

50¢

36¢

70¢

$1.00

COUNTING MONEY

COUNT THE DOLLARS ON THE RIGHT SIDE AND THEN MATCH THEM TO THE ITEMS ON THE LEFT SIDE.

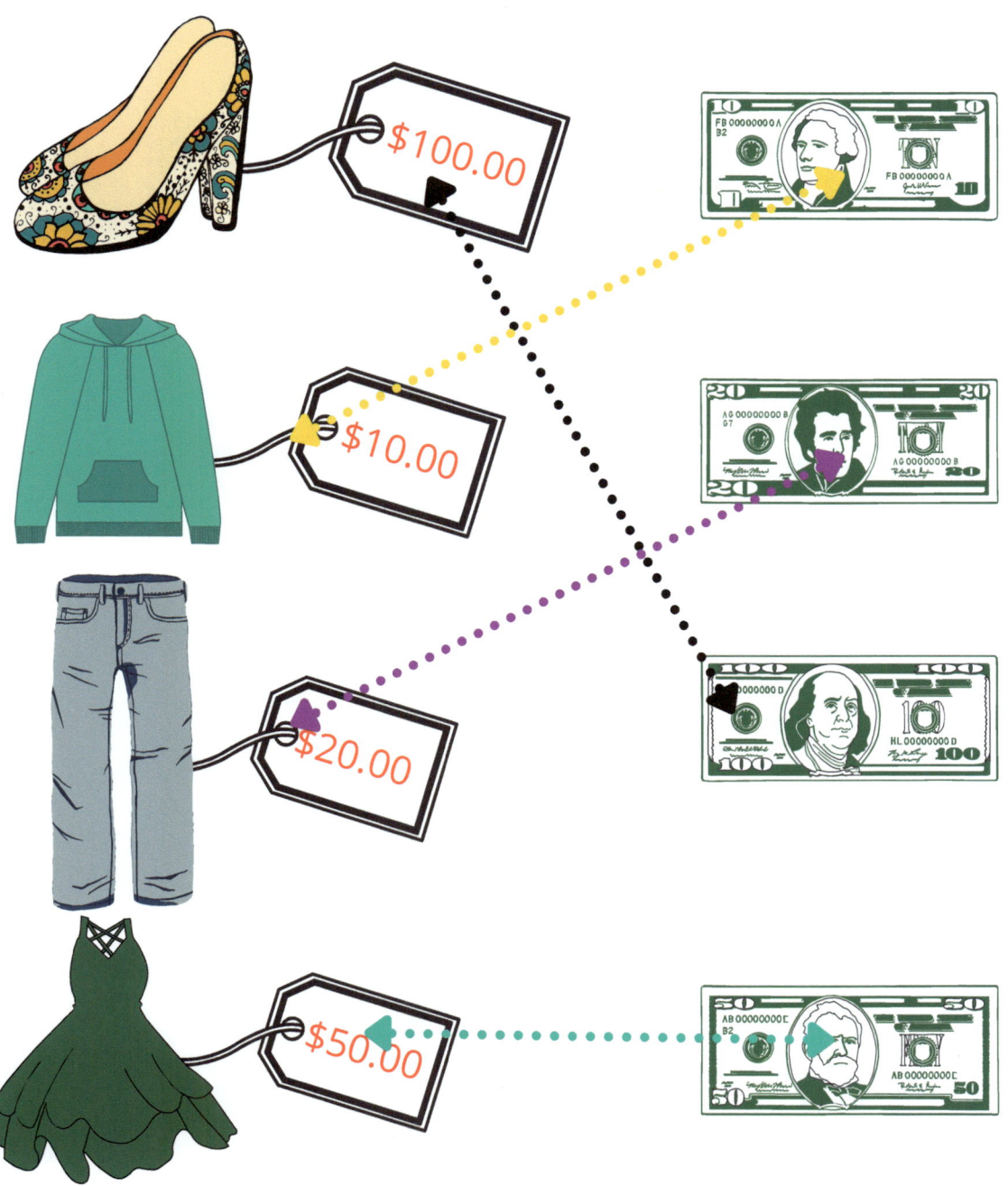

COUNTING MONEY

COUNT THE DOLLARS AND WRITE THE TOTAL AMOUNT

$ **4.00**

$ **16.00**

$ **36.00**

TELLING TIME
ANALOG CLOCKS

WRITE THE TIME ON THE LINES BELOW THE CLOCKS

5:00

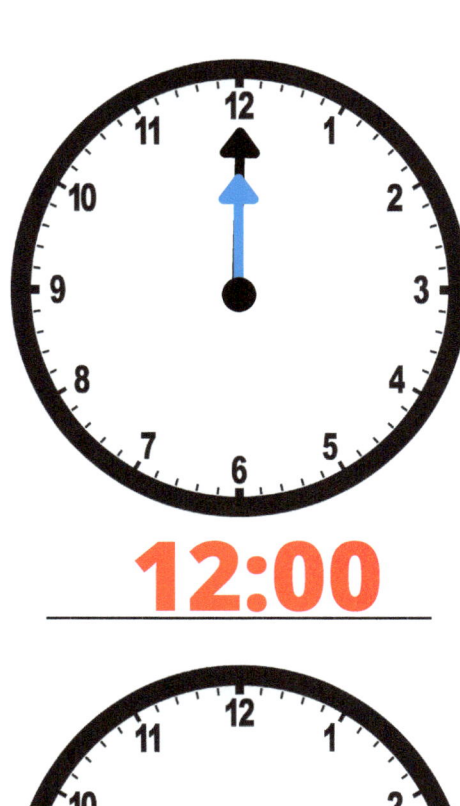

12:00

9:15

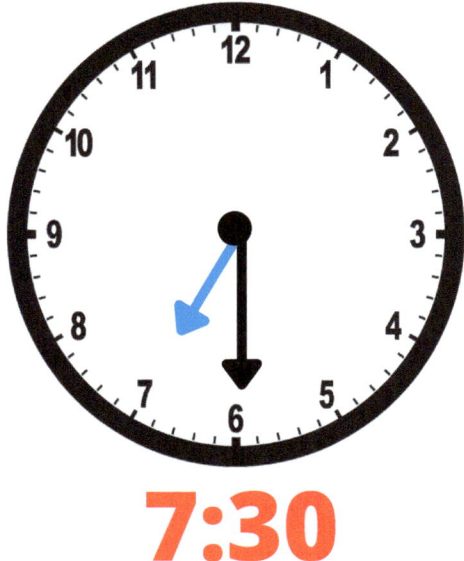

7:30

TELLING TIME

WRITE THE TIME ON THE LINES BELOW THE CLOCKS

3:00

6:15

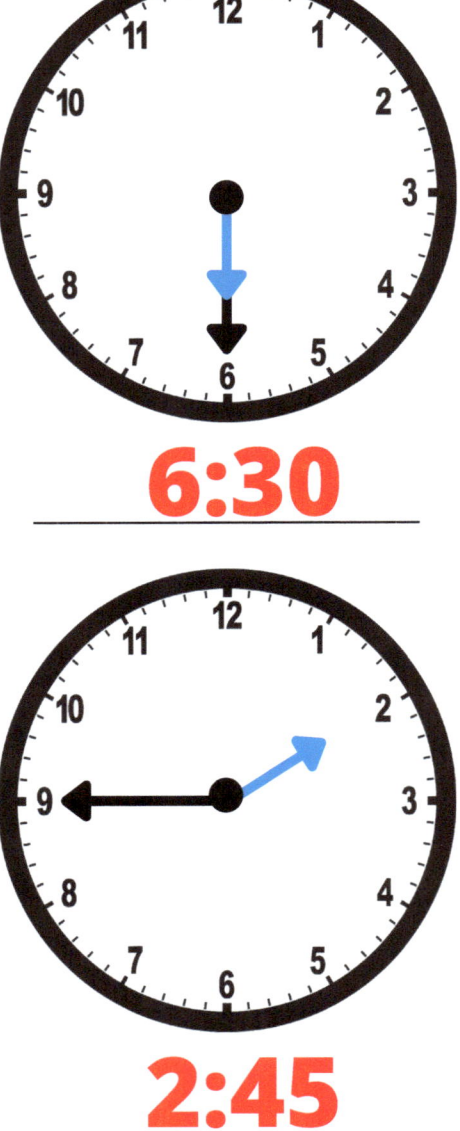

6:30

2:45

TELLING TIME
DIGITAL CLOCK

DIGITAL CLOCKS SHOW THE HOUR BEFORE THE (:) AND THE MINUTES AFTER.
WRITE THE TIME ON THE LINES BELOW THE CLOCKS

2:30

9:00

12:40

1:22